Alfred's Kid's Guitar Course
Movie & TV Songbook
1 & 2

13 Fun Arrangements that Make Learning Even Easier!

Ron Manus • L.C. Harnsberger

Contents

Using the Recording TRACKS 1 & 2

The included **Kid's Guitar Course Movie & TV Songbook recording** contains all the songs in this book for listening and playing along. Use the first two tracks to get your guitar in tune. Listen carefully to the instructions on track 1, then use track 2 to match each string to the recorded pitch. Be sure to tune your guitar every time you play, especially when you play along with the audio.

Stream or download the audio content for this book.
To access online media, visit: **alfred.com/redeem**

Enter the following code:

00-33888_24021771

alfred.com

Printed in USA.

ISBN-10: 0-7390-6419-3 (Book & Online Audio)
ISBN-13: 978-0-7390-6419-1 (Book & Online Audio)

This book is dedicated to Genevieve, Patrese, and Catherine Harnsberger.

Cover illustrations by Jeff Shelly.
Audio recorded at Bar None Studios, Northford, CT
Book interior produced by Workshop Arts, Inc.

The Ballad of Gilligan's Isle

Words and Music by
Sherwood Schwartz
and George Wyle

Track 3

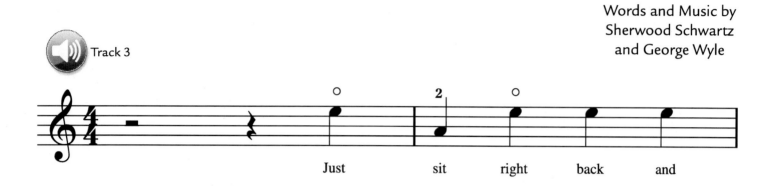

Just sit right back and

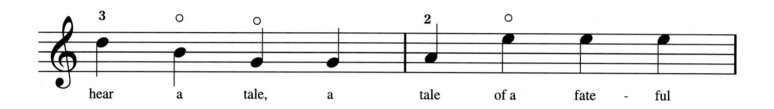

hear a tale, a tale of a fate - ful

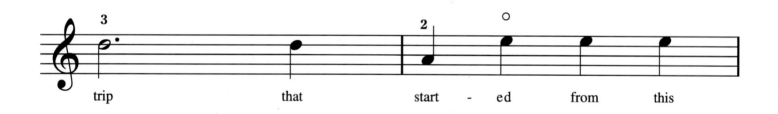

trip that start - ed from this

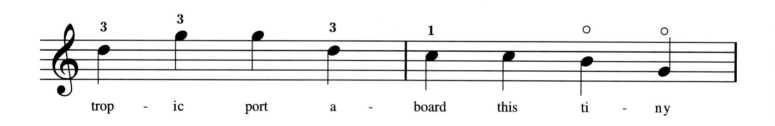

trop - ic port a - board this ti - ny

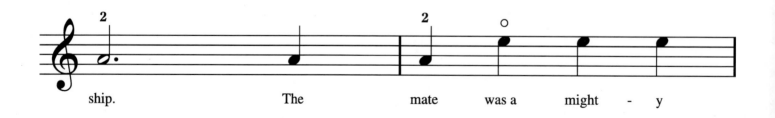

ship. The mate was a might - y

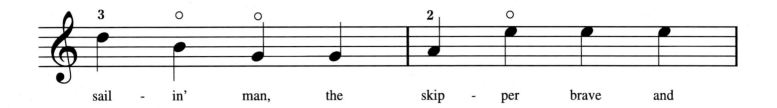

sail - in' man, the skip - per brave and

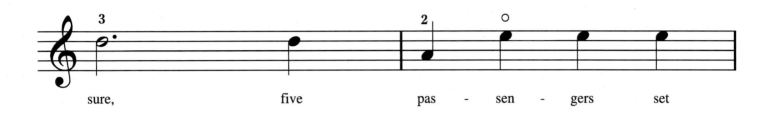

sure, five pas - sen - gers set

sail that day for a three ho - ur

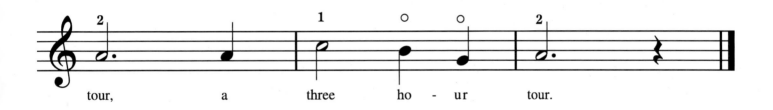

tour, a three ho - ur tour.

Chitty Chitty Bang Bang

Book 1, p. 44 (Complete, p. 70)

Words and Music by
Richard M. Sherman
and Robert B. Sherman

Track 4

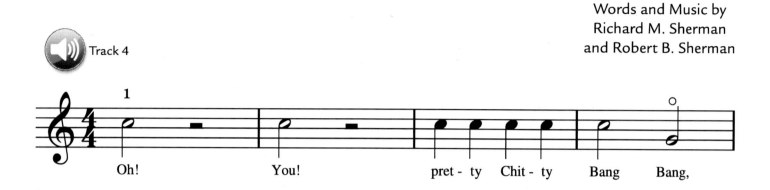

Oh! You! pret - ty Chit - ty Bang Bang,

Chit - ty Chit - ty Bang Bang we love you!

And our pret - ty Chit - ty Bang Bang,

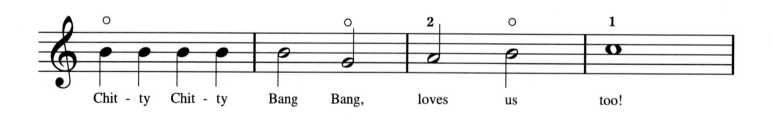

Chit - ty Chit - ty Bang Bang, loves us too!

High! Low! An - y - where we go, on

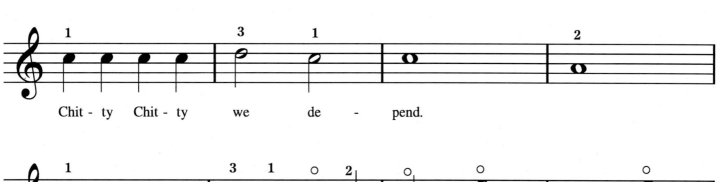

Chit - ty Chit - ty we de - pend.

Bang, Bang Chit - ty Chit - ty Bang Bang, our

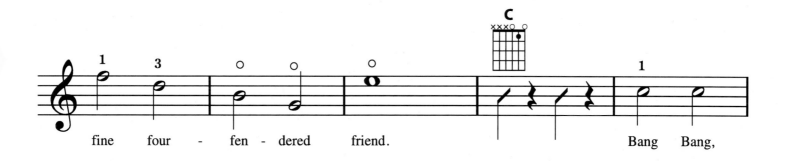

fine four - fen - dered friend. Bang Bang,

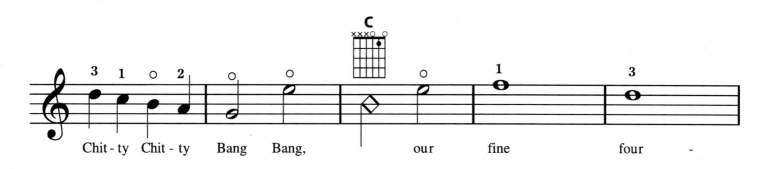

Chit - ty Chit - ty Bang Bang, our fine four -

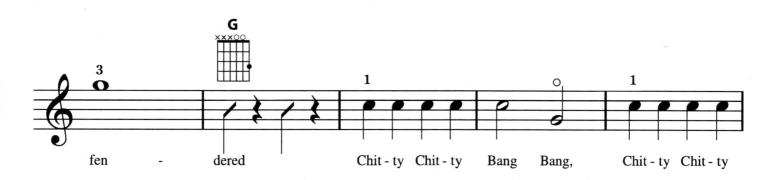

fen - dered Chit - ty Chit - ty Bang Bang, Chit - ty Chit - ty

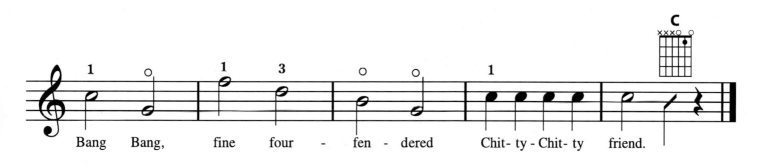

Bang Bang, fine four - fen - dered Chit - ty - Chit- ty friend.

Beauty and the Beast

Lyrics by Howard Ashman
Music by Alan Menken

Track 5

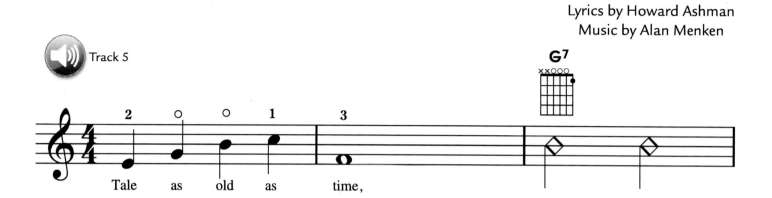

Tale as old as time,

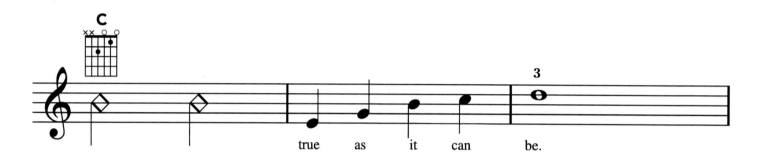

true as it can be.

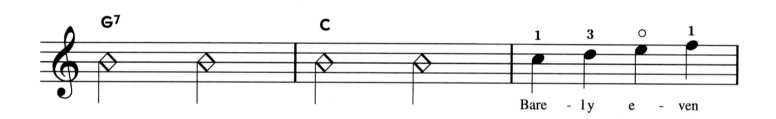

Bare - ly e - ven

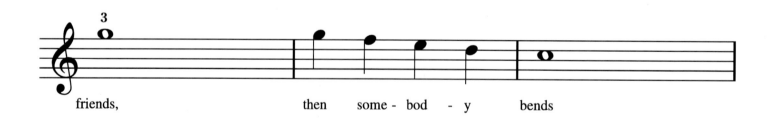

friends, then some - bod - y bends

un - ex - pect - ed ly.

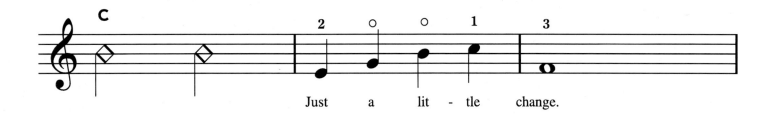

Just a lit - tle change.

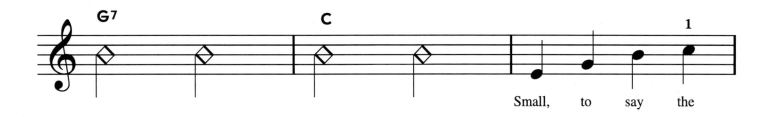

Small, to say the

least. Both a lit - tle scared,

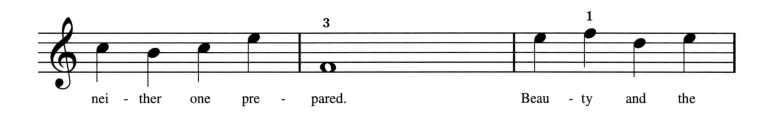

nei - ther one pre - pared. Beau - ty and the

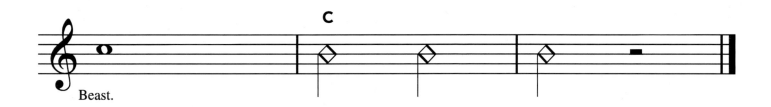

Beast.

You've Got a Friend in Me

Words and Music by
Randy Newman

Track 6

C

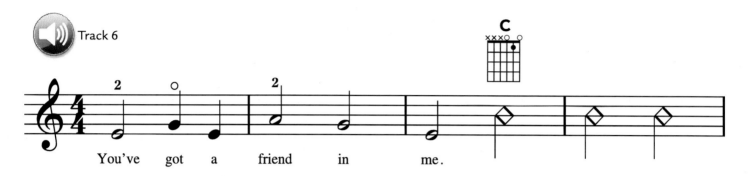

You've got a friend in me.

You've got a friend in me.

C

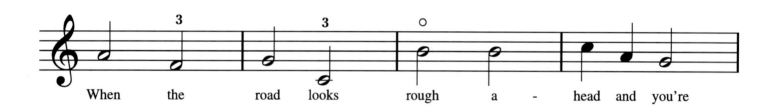

When the road looks rough a - head and you're

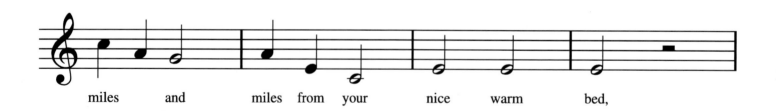

miles and miles from your nice warm bed,

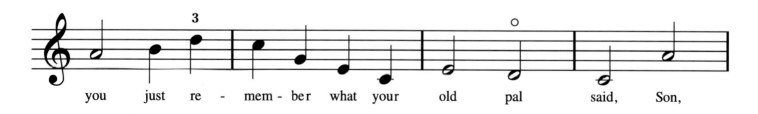

you just re - mem - ber what your old pal said, Son,

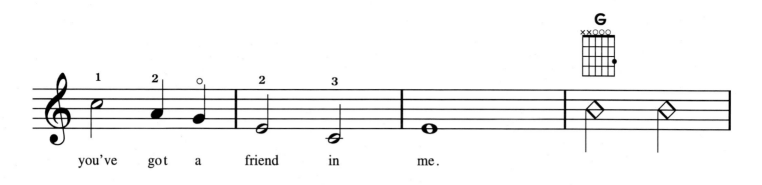

you've got a friend in me.

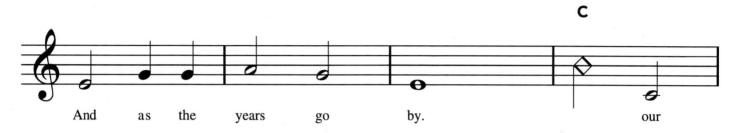

And as the years go by.   our

friend - ship will nev - er die.

You're gon - na see it's our des - ti - ny.

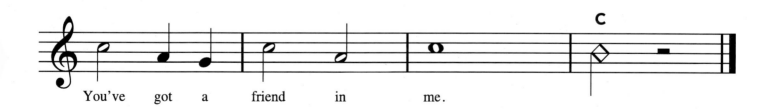

You've got a friend in me.

Raiders March

Track 7

Music by
John Williams

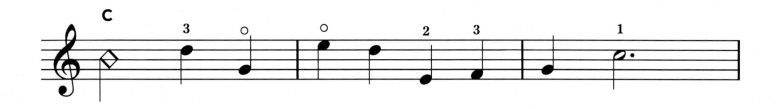

Theme from "Superman"

Music by
John Williams

Track 8

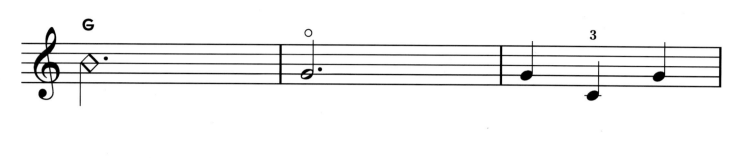

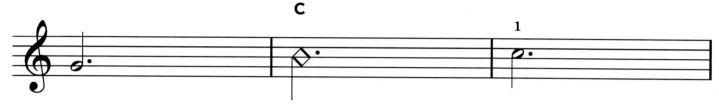

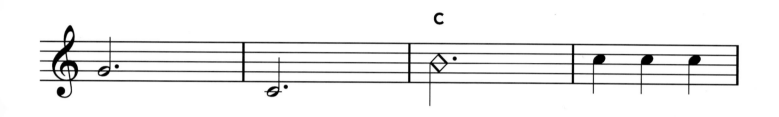

A Whole New World

Words by Tim Rice
Music by Alan Menken

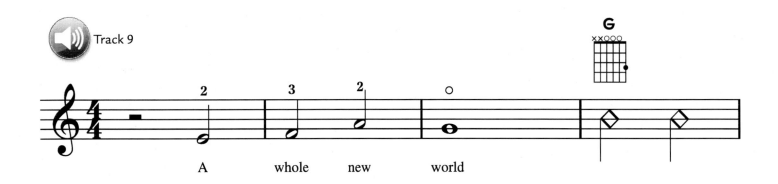

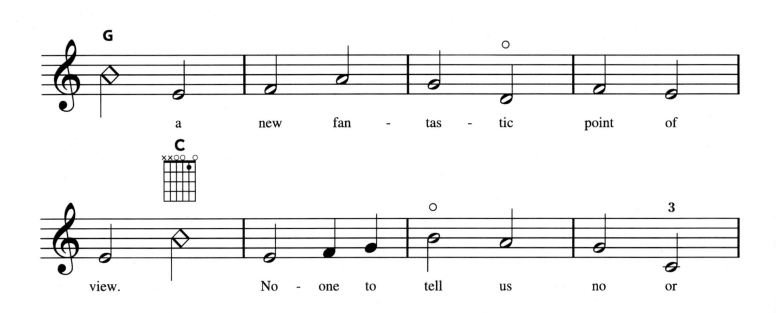

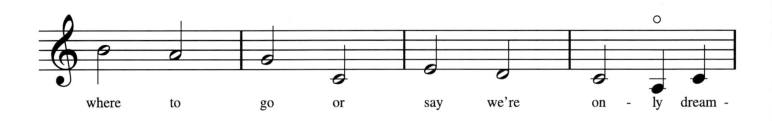

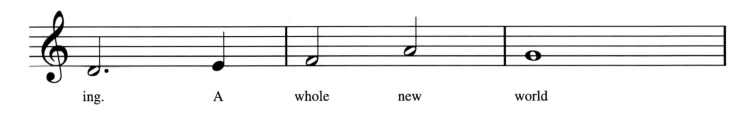

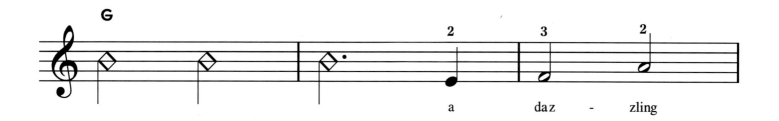

a daz - zling

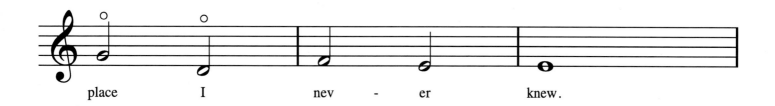

place   I   nev - er   knew.

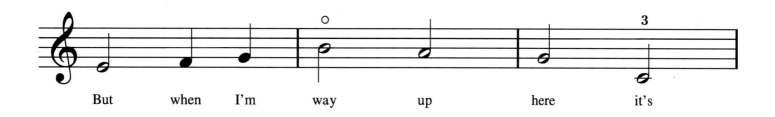

But   when   I'm   way   up   here   it's

crys - tal   clear   that   now   I'm   in   a

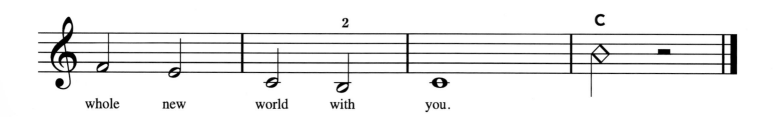

whole   new   world   with   you.

Over the Rainbow

Lyrics by E. Y. Harburg
Music by Harold Arlen

Track 10

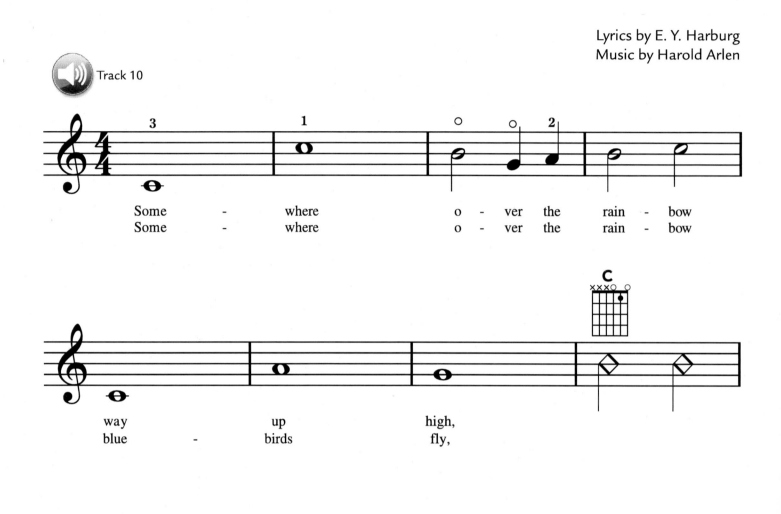

Some - where   o - ver the rain - bow
Some - where   o - ver the rain - bow

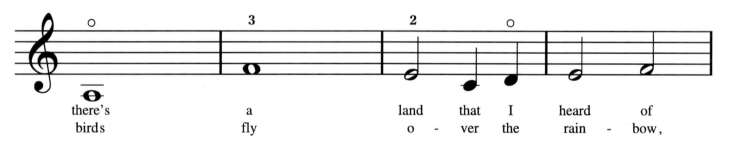

way   up   high,
blue - birds   fly,

there's   a   land that I   heard   of
birds   fly   o - ver the   rain - bow,

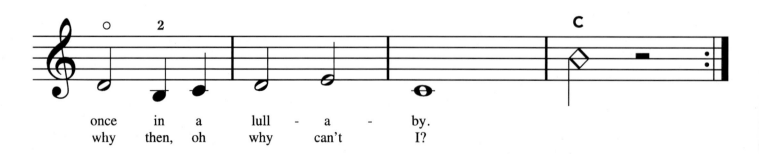

once in a lull - a - by.
why then, oh why can't   I?

Yoda's Theme

Music by
John Williams

Track 11

Fawkes the Phoenix

Book 2, p. 28 (Complete, p. 113)

Music by
John Williams

Track 12

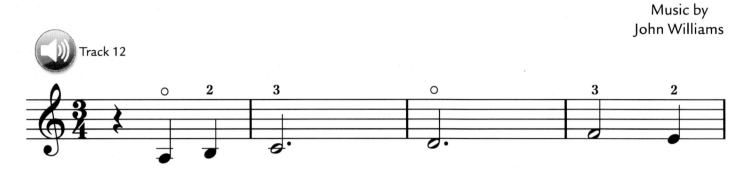

Scooby-Doo, Where Are You?

Words and Music by
David Mook and Ben Raleigh

Track 13

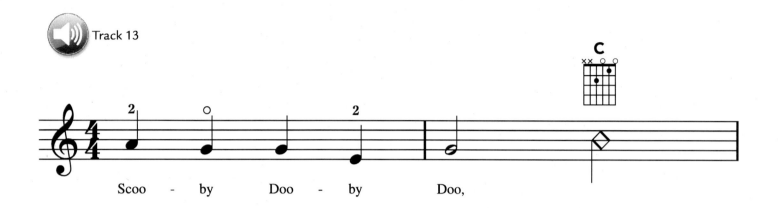

Scoo - by Doo - by Doo,

look - in' for you.

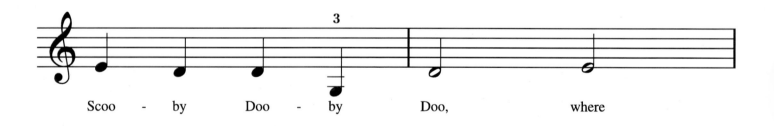

Scoo - by Doo - by Doo, where

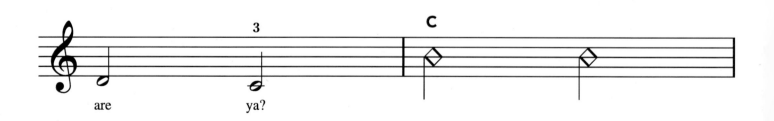

are ya?

All   the   stars   are   here

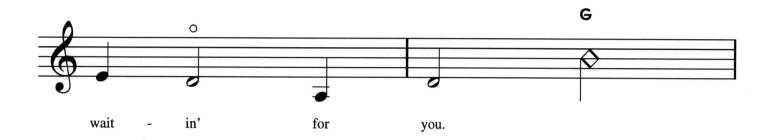

wait - in'   for   you.

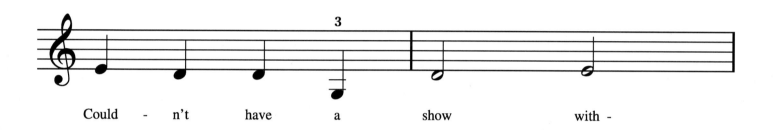

Could - n't   have   a   show   with -

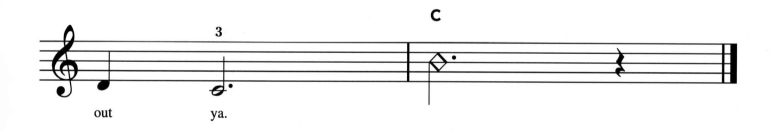

out   ya.

This Is It!

Words and Music by
Mack David and Jerry Livingston

Track 14

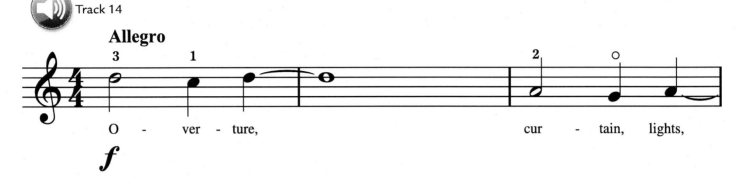

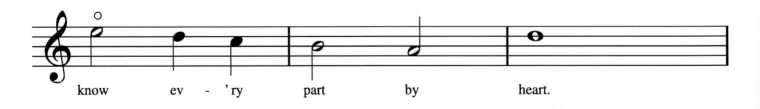

O - ver - ture, curtain lights,

this is it, you'll

hit the heights. And oh, what

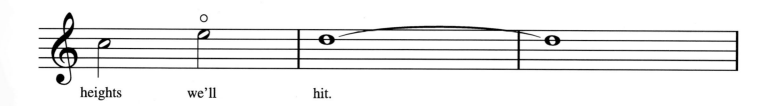

heights we'll hit.

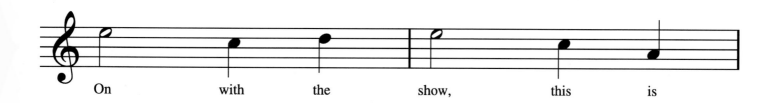

On with the show, this is

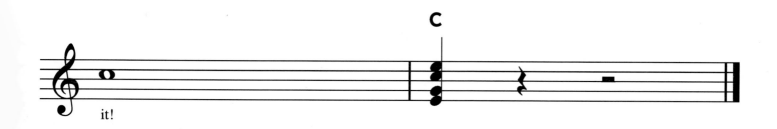

it!

May the Force Be With You

Book 2, p. 44 (Complete, p. 136)

Music by
John Williams

Track 15